learning and study skills program

Level B

INTRODUCTION AND SAMPLE UNIT

NAESP   **nassp**

INTRODUCTION TO THE
hm LEARNING AND STUDY SKILLS PROGRAM:
LEVEL B

Dear Colleague:

The **hm Learning and Study Skills Program: Level B** is designed to provide you with a valuable resource for the teaching of study skills. Please read this Introduction carefully so you can gain a sense of the purposes and values, the means and ends, and the capacities and limitations of this program.

STUDY SKILLS: WHAT ARE THEY?

Study skills are learned abilities that one uses for the purpose of acquiring knowledge and competence. They are specific, observable behaviors that can be described and measured. For example, can a student attend to a set of directions and follow them accurately? Can a student identify the main idea and supporting details? Can a student locate and use information from a table or graph?

Study skills can also be understood as *learning skills,* or *processes for learning.* They are processes that help students to organize and direct the effort they invest in learning. When students learn a study skill, they are learning how to learn more effectively. They are also learning how to take charge of their own learning.

THE hm LEARNING AND STUDY SKILLS PROGRAM: LEVEL B

The **hm Learning and Study Skills Program: Level B** provides an introduction to fundamental study skills for students in grades 3 and 4 through a series of ten activity-oriented units.

The **hm Program** is structured on the assumption that activity-oriented lessons are the most effective way to teach study skills; more succinctly, that "learning by doing" is the best way to develop competence in study skills. The activities in the **hm Program** introduce students to basic learning skills that are useful in a wide variety of learning situations. Students then practice these skills in ways that (1) increase their awareness of the values of these skills and (2) help them become more conscious of themselves as learners.

The **hm Learning and Study Skills Program: Level B** provides you with a focus on the nature and value of skills that can help your students to become more effective learners. It gives you ten initial units for teaching study skills and a great many suggestions for further instruction and reinforcement in each study skill area.

A

The units in the **hm Learning and Study Skills Program: Level B** are:

1. Listening
2. Observing
3. Understanding Directions
4. Categories
5. Put It in Order
6. Tables and Graphs
7. Pictures in Your Mind
8. Main Idea — What's It All About?
9. Problem Solving
10. Problem Solving In Math

THE DEVELOPMENTAL CHARACTER OF THE hm LEARNING AND STUDY SKILLS PROGRAM: LEVEL B

The **hm Learning and Study Skills Program: Level B** is based on a developmental understanding of the capacities and needs of third and fourth graders. Children of these ages think differently than do older children, adolescents, or adults. They tend to be more holistic in their interaction with the world and experience the reality of their imaginations more vividly. They often learn more from observing and listening than they do from reading.

The study skills presented in this **Program** are particularly appropriate for children of these ages. Some of these skills help children use their capacities to listen, observe, and visualize with greater intention and awareness. Other study skills help children begin to develop greater competence in such linear and analytic ways of thinking as sequencing, categorizing, and charting. Finally, children are encouraged to employ this whole repertoire of learning skills as they learn to solve problems more effectively.

STUDY SKILLS AND LEARNING STYLE

Research in cognitive and learning style during the past three decades has demonstrated what perceptive educators have known for a long time: people learn in very different and personal ways. Thus, study skills need to be taught in a way that helps children to value their own learning style(s) as they develop their skills for learning. Such instruction, guided by an awareness of individual differences, will help children to develop study skills that are specifically useful to their own capacities and needs.

The **hm Learning and Study Skills Program: Level B** is grounded in an awareness of learning style as a powerful factor in all learning. Its activities encourage students to find ways of learning that are effective for them as individuals.

USING THE hm LEARNING AND STUDY SKILLS PROGRAM: LEVEL B

WHEN TO TEACH THE PROGRAM

Our field testing of the **hm Program: Level B** has shown that the vast majority of the activities in the **Program** are appropriate for third and fourth graders. However, when you are working with early third graders, you may want to give your students more guidance and take more time for some for some of the exercises.

SEQUENCE OF INSTRUCTION

We have sequenced the ten units in the **Program** in an order that is developmentally sound and effectively balanced in terms of the diversity of the activities within the various units. We recommend that you use the units in the order in which they appear in the **Program.**

If you do choose to teach some units in a different sequence, you will want to keep the following in mind:
* Units 1, 2, and 3 are best taught as a cluster in the order in which they appear in the **Program.** Skills and concepts presented in Units 1 and 2 provide a foundation for the activities in Unit 3.

* Units 4, 5, and 6 are the most academically demanding units and contain more conventional workbook exercises than the other units. You may want to teach these units after your students are comfortable with the **Program's** format.
* Units 9 and 10 tie together many of the skills and concepts presented in the earlier units.

PACING OF INSTRUCTION

No one pacing for the teaching of these units can be recommended for all classes. We have learned from the field test of the **Program** that teachers must pace the use of these units in a way that helps their particular students to acquire competence in the various skills.

A pacing that several of our field testers used with success was to begin a new unit every two weeks. They then used the intervening time to offer ongoing practice of the new study skills.

We recommend that you conduct follow-up activities to help your students develop the study skills introduced to them in each unit. We also urge you *to integrate the practice of study skills into your regular curriculum whenever possible*. The Additional Suggestions provided in the Teacher's Guide at the end of each unit offer activities that can help you accomplish this.

C

PREPARING YOUR STUDENTS

Your students will approach a unit with more direction, confidence, and enthusiasm if you begin the unit by giving them an overview of what they are going to learn. You can usually find one or two key ideas in the unit introduction in the Teacher's Guide that will help you do this. You can also find these key ideas in the Unit Summaries.

SUGGESTED DIRECTIONS

The Teacher's Guide offers Suggested Directions for teaching each unit in the **Program.** Our classroom testing has shown these methods to be useful. Of course, we invite you to adapt them in ways that are most appropriate for your students and your own teaching style.

We suggest that you examine both the Student Text and the Teacher's Guide carefully prior to teaching each unit.

SUGGESTED TIMES

Each section of the Suggested Directions in the Teacher's Guide includes approximate times for the activities within that section. These estimates will help you plan individual lessons or instructional periods. Unit time estimates range from 65-120 minutes. Our field test has demonstrated that 30-40 minutes of working with study skills is a productive amount of time. Thus you will probably need to plan for several blocks of time to complete the activities in most units.

Our classroom testing experience has also shown us that wide variation in teaching style and student levels results in an equally wide variation in the instructional time needed for any one exercise. We suggest that you examine the **Program's** units carefully and gauge your planning of instructional time according to your knowledge of how things actually work in your classroom.

UNIT SUMMARIES

Each unit includes a summary as its final section. While the use of the summaries has not been formally integrated into the Suggested Directions, many teachers have found that the precise wording of these summaries helped students understand what they were learning and why.

ADDITIONAL SUGGESTIONS

Additional Suggestions for each unit are provided in the Teacher's Guide. These suggestions are ideas and activities that build on the skills and concepts introduced in the units. These suggestions provide opportunities for additional practice of the study skills(s) and demonstrate a variety of applications of each new skill. We recommend that you read through the Additional Suggestions prior to teaching a unit. This will give you a better sense of the purpose and direction of the unit.

We suggest that you plan to use some of the relevant suggested activities in the days following your teaching of each of the **Program's** units. You'll want to keep others in mind for use later in the year.

A POTPOURRI OF HINTS AND SUGGESTIONS

USING SMALL GROUPS IN THE CLASSROOM

For some of the activities in the **hm Program,** we have recommended organizing your students into small working groups. We have done this for the following reasons:

(1) Small group processes genuinely engage students in an activity.

(2) Students can share their talents and experience and learn from each other.

(3) Because they offer active participation to each and every student, such processes help both to enhance motivation for learning and increase interest in the content of a lesson.

You may wish to select the membership of the small groups for each exercise based upon your knowledge of your students. Some teachers have found it valuable to maintain fixed groups for periods of time to offer students the experience of developing positive and efficient working relationships.

Individual work is also of critical importance to the learning of study skills. When a skill has been introduced in a group setting, it is necessary to provide for individual work with the skill through other activities.

STUDENT DISCUSSION

Students need the opportunity to discuss their work if they are to learn study skills effectively and know how and when to use them. Their discussion must include not only the "right answer" (if there is one) but also the process through which they arrived at the answer and their reasons for considering it correct. At this point in your students' development of study skills, *the process is more important than the individual answer.* For these reasons, we have included oral activities and the opportunity for small and large group discussion throughout the **Program.**

READING ALOUD DIRECTIONS AND TEXT IN THE STUDENT TEXT

You are instructed to "read aloud and discuss with your students" the directions for many exercises and some sections of text. Some of the written material may be difficult for your students to read independently. Based on your knowledge of your students, you may decide to have them read some directions independently that we have recommended for oral reading. We feel that only you can judge the level of your students' abilities to read various sections of the **Program** to themselves.

In many cases, the directions for a particular exercise printed in the Student Text are augmented by verbal instructions given by the teacher. This is intended to lighten the reading burden on the student for some of the more complex exercises.

You may wish to assess whether your students have understood the directions by asking a student to explain what the class is going to do. If there are further questions, allow another student to respond to them. Listening to both questions and answers will help you see what your students have understood and what might still be unclear to them.

LEARNING STUDY SKILLS: LEARNING FROM ERRORS

An important key to teaching study skills is the recognition that learning a study skill requires most learners to err before they can succeed. We learn skills by being presented with a new skill, trying to use that skill ourselves, committing errors, identifying our errors and then correcting them. Understanding this process creates several responsibilities for the teacher:

(a) The teacher must encourage students to ask questions when they do not understand an idea or directive. Knowing when to ask questions is an important characteristic of the effective learner.

(b) The teacher must provide a space within the learning process where students can try out a new skill, make errors, but not feel that they have failed or are "failures."

(c) The teacher must provide students with enough opportunities for practice of the new skill so that students begin to master the skill and see its usefulness

(d) The teacher must provide usable feedback to students about the effectiveness of their use of the new study skill so that they understand that they can now do certain things that they could not do before.

(e) The teacher must reward students for what they have done well in using the new study skill. With such recognition, students experience success in the learning process, validated both by their own new ability and by the teacher's recognition of this. The experience of success motivates students to continue the development of mastery of the new study skill.

REVIEWING YOUR STUDENTS' WRITTEN WORK

In most instances, the exercises are designed so that students are reviewing and modifying their own work as they proceed through the unit. For these exercises, a cursory review by you while the unit is in progress will be sufficient.

The purpose of the **hm Program** is to encourage your students to develop effective learning skills. The written exercises are not intended to be "tests" of knowledge or mastery. You will want to emphasize to your students that the "worksheets" are intended to help them learn and practice new skills and are not being graded.

ADDITIONAL COMMENTS

The **hm Learning and Study Skills Program: Level B** is designed for use by a teacher in a classroom setting. It is not programmed material that students can work through by themselves, although some of the exercises can be used that way with individual students.

The **hm Learning and Study Skills Program: Level B** incorporates student activity as much as possible, including individual, small group, and whole class activities. This emphasis on activity results from our conviction that people learn skills best by doing.

Some teachers have found the **hm Program** useful as a diagnostic tool. It can show you what your students' current level of competence is and where you need to focus your instructional attention.

We strongly recommend that you tell your students why you think study skills are important in the classroom and in life.

OTHER hm LEARNING AND STUDY SKILLS PROGRAMS

Level A .... Grades 1-2
Level I .... Grades 5-7
Level II .... Grades 8-10
Level III .... Grades 11-13
Math Study Skills .... Grades 6-10
Science Study Skills .... Grades 7-10
GED/Adult Study Skills .... Adult
Workshop Leader's Handbook .... Inservice
Inventory 1 .... Grades 4-7
Inventory 2 .... Grades 8-12
Parent Guide .... Parents

UNIT **5**

Put It In Order

Introduction

In this unit you will be working with **sequence**. Sequence means one thing coming after another in a certain **order**.

Having things in the correct order or sequence is useful. It can help you to organize things and understand them more easily.

There are many ways that things can be put into sequence. Here are a few ways that you might recognize:

- from shortest to tallest;

- from heaviest to lightest;

- from easiest to hardest;

- from most important to least important.

25

SUGGESTED DIRECTIONS FOR UNIT 5

1. Begin by telling your students that they will be talking about *order* or *sequence*. Use the words interchangeably throughout the unit.

    Read aloud and discuss with your students the **Introduction** (page 25). Point out to your students that this type of ordering can be done in either direction. For example, "from tallest to shortest" could be "from shortest to tallest." You might also want to brainstorm with your students other things that could be ordered in these ways.

    Approximate Time: 5 MINUTES

I

Think About It

We depend on many things being in the correct **order** or **sequence** everyday. Look at the clock below. If this clock were hanging up in your classroom, you would not be able to use it to tell time. The numbers have to be in a particular order or sequence for the clock to be useful.

Or, think about a calendar like the one below. The days and dates have to come one after another in a certain order or sequence for the calendar to be useful.

Monday	Tuesday	Saturday	Friday	Sunday	Wednesday	Thursday
		2	7	11	4	5
9	8	6	1	10	3	14
12	16	19	21	13	22	20
15	23	25	14	18	27	28
30	24	29	17	26		

But when does school vacation start?

26

2. Read aloud and discuss with your students **Think About It** (page 26). Help your students to see that when the numbers on the clock are out of sequence, and the days and the dates are in no special order on the calendar, the clock and calendar are not useful.

5 MINUTES

Exercise 1

Directions: Each of the lists of words, numbers, or patterns below are in some kind of sequence. One item in each list has been left out. Circle the correct answer below each list that correctly completes each sequence.

EXAMPLE: 1, 2, 3, __, 5

     6   7 ④ 5 9

1. 101, 102, 103, _____, 105

   100   104   106   10001

2. April, May, June, _____, August

   September   January   July   March

3. _____, 6:00 pm, 7:00 pm, 8:00 pm, 9:00 pm

   10:00 pm   5:00 am   5:00 pm   4:00 pm

4. poor, fair, good, very good, _____

   cheap   correct   happy   excellent

5. hot, _____, cool, cold, frozen

   warm   slippery   pretty   comfortable

6. tiny, _____, medium, big, gigantic

   weird   silly   small   magnificent

7. Anna, Barbara, _____, David, Evan

   Jamal   LeRoy   Will   Carole

8.

3. Read aloud and discuss with your students the directions and example for **Exercise I** (page 27). Have them complete the exercise independently. When your students have finished, go over the exercise orally. Help your students see that when they complete a sequence, they are recognizing a pattern.

Fourth grade teachers may find their students ready to understand that *some sequences are reversible.* 5 – 4 – 3 – 2 – 1 is as valid a sequence as 1 – 2 – 3 – 4 – 5.

10 MINUTES

4. For a follow-up discussion to **Exercise 1,** hold up a list of the classroom members that is in random order. Ask your students what different ways the names could be *ordered*. They may suggest height, age, alphabetically by first name, or alphabetically by last name. Explain how alphabetizing class lists by last name makes it easier for you to keep track of your students' work, grades, attendance at school, milk or lunch orders, and so forth.

5 MINUTES

Exercise 2

Directions: Sometimes a group of words or ideas needs to be in a certain order; sometimes it does not. Look at the six lists below. Circle the lists that **are** in some kind of order.

1
DAYS OF THE WEEK

Sunday
Monday
Tuesday
Wednesday
Thursday
Friday
Saturday

2
BIG TOE SOCCER TEAM

Johnny Kicker
Paula Punt
Stubby Toe
Fast Ricky
Slow Sam
Barbara Boot
Racey Ray
Fabulous Fran
Mad Melvin
Daring Dave
Mighty Maria

3
SCHOOLS IN DISTRICT #3

Booksville Middle School
A. E. Newman High School
Funnybone Elementary
Wonderkid Elementary

4
TOP TIMES FOR 1 MILE RUN

Olivia	5 min. 40 sec.
Gordon	5 min. 55 sec.
Linda	6 min. 10 sec.
Bob	6 min. 30 sec.
Susan	6 min. 45 sec.
David	7 min. 5 sec.

5
MORNING SCHEDULE

8:30	Opening Exercise
8:45	Reading
10:15	Recess
10:45	Math
12:00	Lunch

6
MAJOR NEWSPAPERS IN TOWN

City News
Bigtown Bugle
The Morning Times
The Evening Press

28

5. Read and discuss with your students the directions to **Exercise 2** (page 28). First, allow them time to review and think about the lists. Then ask your students which lists are in a particular order or sequence. After your students have identified lists #1, #4, and #5 as having a clearcut order or sequence, return to the list #1 and ask:

"In list #1, why is it important to have the days of the week in a particular order?" (Accept plausible answers.)

"In list #4, why is it useful to have the times it took different people to run a mile in the order that they are in?" (There is a wide range of acceptable answers for lists #4 and #5.)

"In list #5, why is it useful to have the morning schedule presented in the order it is in?"

You may want to ask your students how they think the *sequence* in any of these lists might be varied, especially for the three lists where the items are not now ordered.

10 MINUTES

Exercise 3

Directions: You have been visited by the greatest of all Fairy Godmothers. She has granted you the fantasy birthday of a lifetime. Anything you want is yours for the asking. You can ask for something for you alone, something you share, or something for your family.

On the lines below, list 5 things that you would like to have or have happen for this birthday.

BIRTHDAY WISH LIST

_____

_____

_____

_____

_____

29

6. Read aloud and discuss with your students the directions to **Exercise 3** (page 29). Advise them that spelling is not important and that they should limit each item to two or three words. For example, "a trip to Disneyland" can be briefly written as "Disneyland." Have your students complete their lists individually.

5-8 MINUTES

O

How Important Is It?

You can make another kind of **sequence** by putting things **in order of importance**. Whenever you make a decision to do one thing instead of another, you are putting things in order of their importance to you.

Exercise 4

Directions: The Fairy Godmother now reports that there is a shortage of wishes. She says that you might not get all of your wishes. You are going to have to decide which wishes you want to have most.

On the lines below, list your same 5 choices from Exercise III. This time, put them in order of the ones you want the most. Number #1 will be the wish that you just don't want to give up. Number #2 will be the next most important wish to you. Number #5 will be the one it is easiest for you to give up.

BIRTHDAY WISH LIST

1. _____

2. _____

3. _____

4. _____

5. _____

30

7. Read aloud and discuss with your students **How Important Is It?** and the directions to **Exercise 4** (page 30). Have them complete their lists individually.

8-10 MINUTES

8. Now tell your students that word has come in that they'll only get their first three wishes. Ask your students to share their top three choices with the class.

8 MINUTES

> In **Exercise 4** you are addressing the practice of *prioritizing* without actually using that word. Before doing this exercise, you may want to introduce this concept to your students by asking them if they can recall a situation where there were two things that they very much wanted to do and had to choose just one.

Exercise 5

Directions: In this exercise you and a partner are going to tell a story. All the sentences that you need for your story are listed below. The sentences are about a woman and her dog. The sentences are not in any special order. You will only use **some** of them.

First read through all of the sentences. Then work with your partner to choose 10 of these sentences to put into **a sequence that tells a story**. Number the sentences you choose from 1 to 10 to help you plan the order of the story.

Then write your sentences, in the order that you numbered them, on the lines at the bottom of this page. The first sentence of the story has already been chosen.

___ They went down the street.   ___ They saw an old house.

___ The house looked empty.   ___ They heard a groaning sound.

___ The dog pulled her forward.   ___ They ran away as fast as possible.

___ The dog tugged hard on the leash.   ___ They never went there again.

___ She shouted, "Let's get going!"   ___ The dog was not scared.

___ The scary sounds got louder.   ___ The woman was scared.

___ They went inside.   ___ He sniffed at the front door.

___ They went up on the porch.   ___ A woman and her dog went for a walk.

1. <u>A woman and her dog went for a walk.</u>

2. _____

3. _____

4. _____

5. _____

6. _____

7. _____

8. _____

9. _____

10. _____

31

9. Make sure that your students have a pencil and an eraser. Organize your students into pairs. Tell them that they will complete **Exercise 5** by working with their partners. Encourage your students to discuss their story sequences with their partners as they work. Have all students record their sequences in their *own* texts.

Read aloud and discuss with your students the directions to **Exercise 5** (page 31). In addition to the directions in the Student Text, point out the following to your students:

- They might have to number and re-number their selected sentences in order to get the sequence they want.

- Although some combinations may be more sensible than others, many acceptable sequences are possible.

- There are additional lines if anyone wants to use more than ten sentences.

Unit 5 Summary: *Put It In Order*

Sequence means one thing coming after another in a certain order.

Some things can be **ordered** or **sequenced** in more than one way.

Things or ideas often **make more sense** when they are organized in the correct sequence or order.

Things or ideas are often **more useful** when they are organized in the correct sequence or order.

You can order things in a way that shows what is most important to you.

32

Allow some time for story sequences to be shared aloud by those students who wish to do so.

15-20 MINUTES

ADDITIONAL SUGGESTIONS FOR UNIT 5

1. As an introductory activity to demonstrate how sequence can affect meaning, write the following sentences on the chalkboard:

   <u>Only</u> Dad washed his son's shirt.

   Dad <u>only</u> washed his son's shirt.

   Dad washed <u>only</u> his son's shirt.

   Dad washed his <u>only</u> son's shirt.

   Dad washed his son's <u>only</u> shirt.

   Dad washed his son's shirt <u>only</u>.

   Read these sentences with the correct intonation so that your students hear the change in meaning. Discuss with your students how the position of the word *only* has altered the meaning of the basic sentence.

2. Along the same lines as the activity above, present to your class a list of events (as in a story) in a particular sequence. Examine with your students how the outcome might differ if the order of these events were changed in various ways. This activity can also be done with a sequence of steps in a procedure, such as a recipe.

3. Cut up picture frames from a comic strip, and ask your students to arrange them in the proper sequence. Two variations of this idea are:

   a. Black out the captions in the comic strip frames to allow for more variety in possible sequences.

   b. Allow students to create alternative sequences by giving them one or two additional blank frames with which to make their own pictures to insert into the comic strip sequence.

4. Order in time is an understanding that takes years for children to acquire. Make a historical time-line around the perimeter of the room that will stay up for the entire year. Have it begin with a year that is appropriate to your curriculum and extend to the present year. Have students label important events that they encounter in all areas of study. You might start out with their birthdates and those of their favorite authors or famous persons. You will find that students will eagerly research dates such as when the school was built or when people first landed on the moon, so they can make regular contributions to the time-line.

5. The *flowchart* is an excellent device to illustrate sequence. Flowcharts can be used to depict a story sequence, a science procedure, or a plan of action. Shown below is an entertaining flowchart activity to help your students think about sequence. Give your students a copy of this flowchart with some or all of the connecting arrows omitted. Ask them to write in the missing arrows to correctly complete the sequence. After considerable practice with this kind of activity, students can enjoy creating their own flowcharts for others to complete.

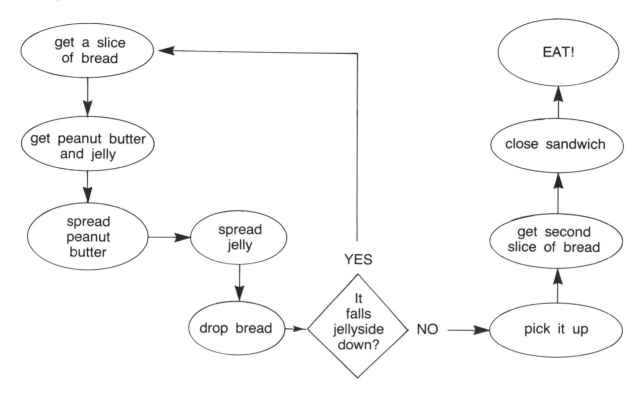

6. **Exercise 5** can be used as valuable pre-writing activity. Before writing a story, ask your students to brainstorm a list of simple sentences that pertain to their story idea. Encourage them to write anything that comes to mind. Then have your students review their lists and order those sentences that they want to use. Using this sequence as a skeleton, they can add details and embellish the language to create a finished story.

7. When working in different subject areas, take the time to help your students recognize where sequence is important. Some examples of this are steps in a science experiment; steps in a classroom schedule; steps in solving a math problem or algorithm; and events in a story.

8. Help your students learn to identify time qualifiers in written text. Some examples of words that cue the reader to order are the following:

while	during	after	already
before	as	following	until
now	then	next	later
soon	finally	when	in the meantime

NOTES

Put It In Order

Introduction

In this unit you will be working with **sequence**. Sequence means one thing coming after another in a certain **order**.

Having things in the correct order or sequence is useful. It can help you to organize things and understand them more easily.

There are many ways that things can be put into sequence. Here are a few ways that you might recognize:

- from shortest to tallest;

- from heaviest to lightest;

- from easiest to hardest;

- from most important to least important.

5

Think About It

We depend on many things being in the correct **order** or **sequence** everyday. Look at the clock below. If this clock were hanging up in your classroom, you would not be able to use it to tell time. The numbers have to be in a particular order or sequence for the clock to be useful.

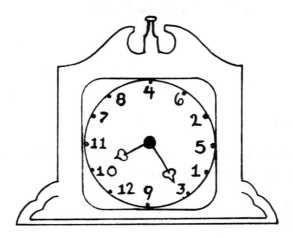

Or, think about a calendar like the one below. The days and dates have to come one after another in a certain order or sequence for the calendar to be useful.

5

Monday	Tuesday	Saturday	Friday	Sunday	Wednesday	Thursday
		2	7	11	4	5
9	8	6	1	10	3	14
12	16	19	21	13	22	20
15	23	25	14	18	27	28
30	24	29	17	26		

But when does school vacation start?

Exercise 1

Directions: Each of the lists of words, numbers, or patterns below are in some kind of sequence. One item in each list has been left out. Circle the correct answer below each list that correctly completes each sequence.

EXAMPLE: 1, 2, 3, __, 5

6   7   ④   5   9

1. 101, 102, 103, _____, 105

   100   104   106   10001

2. April, May, June, _____, August

   September   January   July   March

3. _____, 6:00 pm, 7:00 pm, 8:00 pm, 9:00 pm

   10:00 pm   5:00 am   5:00 pm   4:00 pm

4. poor, fair, good, very good, _____

   cheap   correct   happy   excellent

5. hot, _____, cool, cold, frozen

   warm   slippery   pretty   comfortable

6. tiny, _____, medium, big, gigantic

   weird   silly   small   magnificent

7. Anna, Barbara, _____, David, Evan

   Jamal   LeRoy   Will   Carole

8.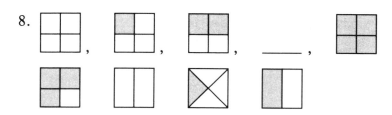

5

Exercise 2

Directions: Sometimes a group of words or ideas needs to be in a certain order; sometimes it does not. Look at the six lists below. Circle the lists that **are** in some kind of order.

1

DAYS OF THE WEEK

Sunday
Monday
Tuesday
Wednesday
Thursday
Friday
Saturday

2

BIG TOE SOCCER TEAM

Johnny Kicker
Paula Punt
Stubby Toe
Fast Ricky
Slow Sam
Barbara Boot
Racey Ray
Fabulous Fran
Mad Melvin
Daring Dave
Mighty Maria

3

SCHOOLS IN DISTRICT #3

Booksville Middle School
A. E. Newman High School
Funnybone Elementary
Wonderkid Elementary

4

TOP TIMES FOR 1 MILE RUN

Olivia	5 min. 40 sec.
Gordon	5 min. 55 sec.
Linda	6 min. 10 sec.
Bob	6 min. 30 sec.
Susan	6 min. 45 sec.
David	7 min. 5 sec.

5

MORNING SCHEDULE

8:30	Opening Exercise
8:45	Reading
10:15	Recess
10:45	Math
12:00	Lunch

6

MAJOR NEWSPAPERS IN TOWN

City News
Bigtown Bugle
The Morning Times
The Evening Press

Exercise 3

Directions: You have been visited by the greatest of all Fairy Godmothers. She has granted you the fantasy birthday of a lifetime. Anything you want is yours for the asking. You can ask for something for you alone, something you share, or something for your family.

On the lines below, list 5 things that you would like to have or have happen for this birthday.

BIRTHDAY WISH LIST

_____

_____

_____

_____

_____

5

AA

How Important Is It?

You can make another kind of **sequence** by putting things **in order of importance**. Whenever you make a decision to do one thing instead of another, you are putting things in order of their importance to you.

Exercise 4

Directions: The Fairy Godmother now reports that there is a shortage of wishes. She says that you might not get all of your wishes. You are going to have to decide which wishes you want to have most.

On the lines below, list your same 5 choices from Exercise III. This time, put them in order of the ones you want the most. Number #1 will be the wish that you just don't want to give up. Number #2 will be the next most important wish to you. Number #5 will be the one it is easiest for you to give up.

BIRTHDAY WISH LIST

5

1. _____

2. _____

3. _____

4. _____

5. _____

Exercise 5

Directions: In this exercise you and a partner are going to tell a story. All the sentences that you need for your story are listed below. The sentences are about a woman and her dog. The sentences are not in any special order. You will only use **some** of them.

First read through all of the sentences. Then work with your partner to choose 10 of these sentences to put into **a sequence that tells a story.** Number the sentences you choose from 1 to 10 to help you plan the order of the story.

Then write your sentences, in the order that you numbered them, on the lines at the bottom of this page. The first sentence of the story has already been chosen.

___ They went down the street.

___ The house looked empty.

___ The dog pulled her forward.

___ The dog tugged hard on the leash.

___ She shouted, "Let's get going!"

___ The scary sounds got louder.

___ They went inside.

___ They went up on the porch.

___ They saw an old house.

___ They heard a groaning sound.

___ They ran away as fast as possible.

___ They never went there again.

___ The dog was not scared.

___ The woman was scared.

___ He sniffed at the front door.

___ A woman and her dog went for a walk.

1. A woman and her dog went for a walk.

2. _____

3. _____

4. _____

5. _____

6. _____

7. _____

8. _____

9. _____

10. _____

5

Unit 5 Summary: *Put It In Order*

Sequence means one thing coming after another in a certain order.

Some things can be **ordered** or **sequenced** in more than one way.

Things or ideas often **make more sense** when they are organized in the correct sequence or order.

Things or ideas are often **more useful** when they are organized in the correct sequence or order.

You can order things in a way that shows what is most important to you.

hm Learning And Study Skills Program

Level A	Grades 1-2
Level B	Grades 3-4
Level I	Grades 5-7
Level II	Grades 8-10
Level III	Grades 11-13
Math Study Skills	Grades 6-10
Science Study Skills	Grades 7-10
GED/Adult Study Skills	Adult
Workshop Leader's Handbook	Inservice
Inventory 1	Grades 4-7
Inventory 2	Grades 8-12
Parent Guide	Parents

For further information contact:
hm Learning and Study Skills/NASSP
P.O. Box 95010
Newton, MA 02195
Tel: (617) 965-0048
FAX: (617) 965-0056

0-8108-3849-4
Scarecrow Press
1-800-462-6420
717-794-3800